This IS WHAT I EAT

All rights reserved. Published in the United States by Rodale Kids, an imprint of
Random House Children's Books, a division of Penguin Random House LLC, New York.

Rodale and the colophon are registered trademarks and Rodale Kids is a trademark
of Penguin Random House LLC.

Visit us on the Web! rhcbooks.com

Educators and librarians, for a variety of teaching tools, visit us at RHTeachersLibrarians.com

Library of Congress Cataloging-in-Publication Data is available upon request.
ISBN 978-0-593-30929-2 (trade)

The artist created the illustrations for this book digitally in Procreate.
The text of this book is set in 16-point Apercu.
Book design by Jan Gerardi

MANUFACTURED IN CHINA
10 9 8 7 6 5 4 3 2 1
First Edition

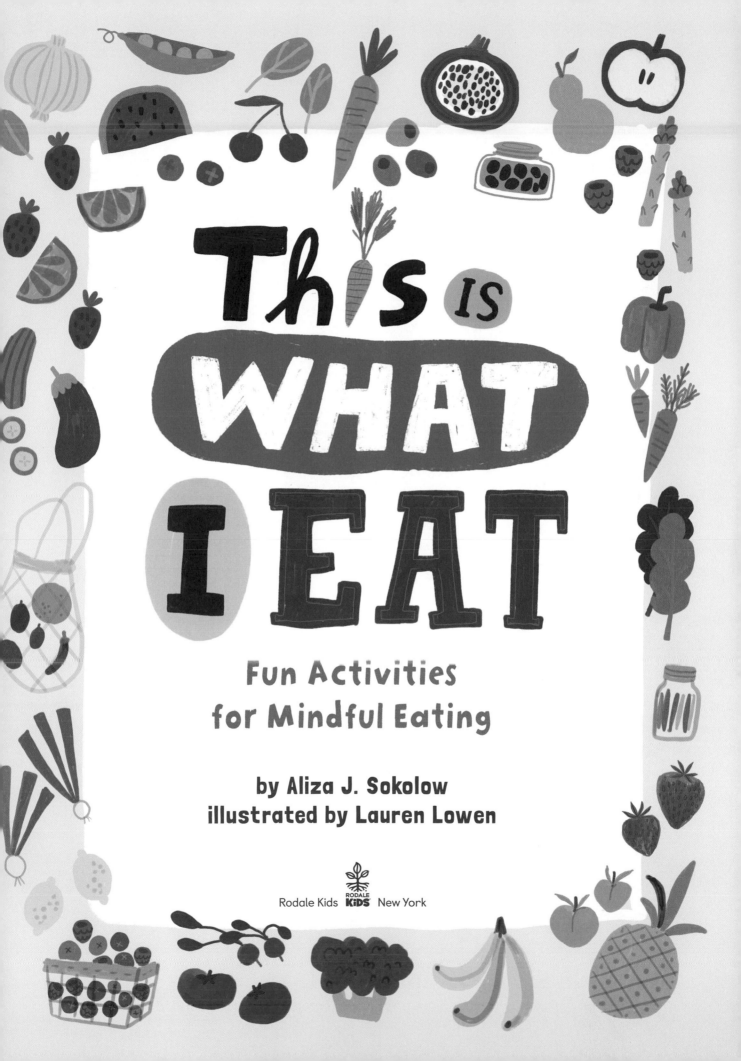

This IS WHAT I EAT

Fun Activities for Mindful Eating

by Aliza J. Sokolow

illustrated by Lauren Lowen

Rodale Kids New York

Hi! Welcome to your book about what you eat!

Let's get to know each other.

Hello! My name is _____.

I live in _____.

Circle the answers that apply to you!

My favorite color is

ORANGE RED GREEN
PURPLE BLUE
YELLOW PINK

just like

CHILI PEPPERS
RADISHES
PEAS
BLUE POTATOES
PEPPERS
ONIONS
PURPLE CABBAGE

I also love

ORANGE RED GREEN
PURPLE BLUE
YELLOW PINK

which is the color of

ORANGES
EGGPLANT
KIWI
BANANAS
BLUEBERRIES
DRAGON FRUITS
APPLES

Food is my favorite thing in the whole world!
Want to know why? Well, there are
SO MANY REASONS!

Check all the reasons **YOU** love food.

It gives me energy to play!

It keeps me healthy!

It's delicious!

LET'S PLAY

LEMONADE
25¢

yummy!

I enjoy eating with family and friends!

Celebrations!

It just makes me happy!

Food makes the world go round!

I have a little secret. Not many people believe it at first . . .
but a lot of the YUMMiEST, best food comes from the ground!
I'll show you.

INTRO TO FRUITS AND VEGGIES

First, let's get this out of the way:
Food from the **GROUND** doesn't taste
like **DIRT** or **ROCKS** or **LEAVES**!

(Definitely don't try *those* at home!)

Foodie Fact!

Besides growing from the ground, fruits and
veggies also grow on trees and in bushes!

What face would you make if you ate something icky?
Draw it below.

YUCK!

We're talking  and VEGGIES!

Fruits and veggies come in all sorts of flavors, so even if you don't like brussels sprouts, you might like:

You're sure to find the right food for you.

Can you draw lines to match the fruits and veggies to their FLAVORS?

Sweet

Sour/Tart

Spicy

Bitter

And to their TEXTURES?

Crunchy

Creamy

Spiky

Squishy

Do you already have a favorite fruit or veggie?
Don't answer yet! First, we're going to
meet some of my friends.

POMEGRANATE
SEEDS

BLUEBERRY

MANGO

PEPPER

TURNIP

GRAPEFRUIT

PAPAYA

COCONUT

JACKFRUIT

PUMPKIN

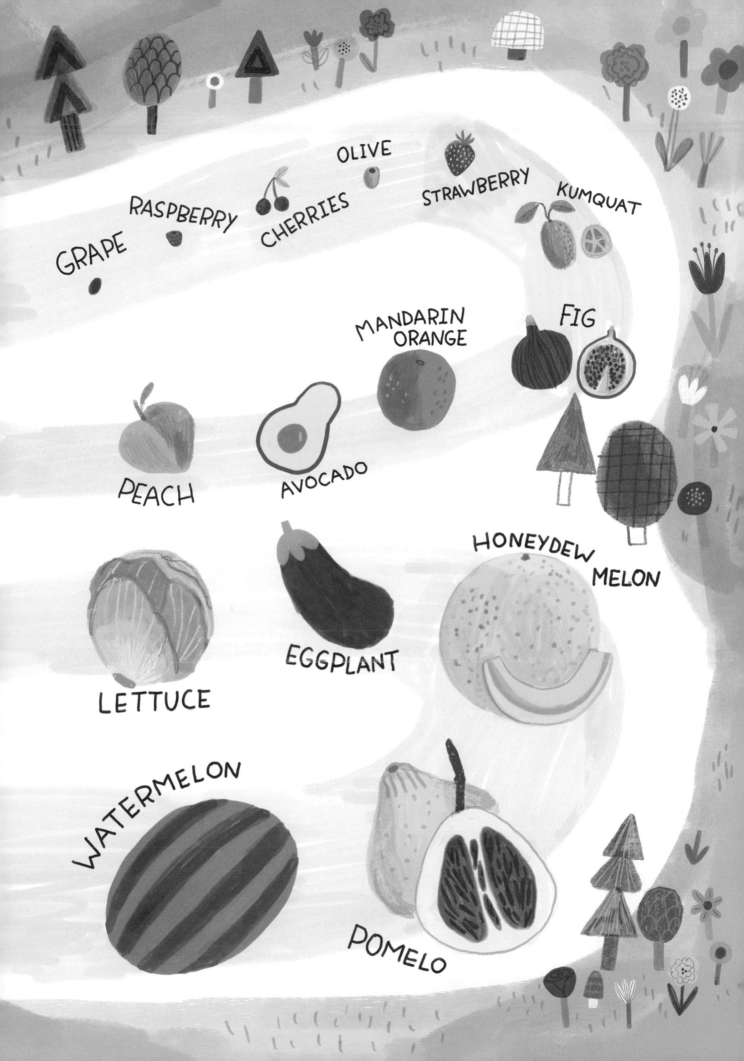

GRAPE

RASPBERRY

CHERRIES

OLIVE

STRAWBERRY

KUMQUAT

FIG

MANDARIN ORANGE

PEACH

AVOCADO

HONEYDEW MELON

LETTUCE

EGGPLANT

WATERMELON

POMELO

Fruits and veggies come in all sorts of SHAPES and SIZES.

Some are round like a hug, and others have spikes, humps, and bumps!

Some need their skins sliced off, others need to be peeled . . .

. . . and others are ready to eat!

It's not what's outside that counts, but what's inside our fruits and vegetables—just like with you!

You know those perfectly shaped fruits and veggies you see at the shop? Plants don't always grow that way!

The not-so-secret secret is that they taste the same no matter how they look! (And sometimes the oddball tastes even better.)

Now it's your turn!
Draw a "perfect-looking" fruit or veggie . . .

then draw a wacky-looking one!

One of my favorite things about fruits and veggies
is that they come in every COLOR.
Food is more FUN when it makes a rainbow!

PINK

RED

ORANGE

YELLOW

Some foods, such as apples and carrots, come in a bunch of colors. Some, such as tomatoes and peppers, change colors as they grow! Color all the different fruits and vegetables you see.

PURPLE

Foodie Fact!

Did you know that apples come in 7,500 varieties? They vary in color (on the inside and outside), texture (ranging from mushy to crispy), and flavor (from sweet to tart).

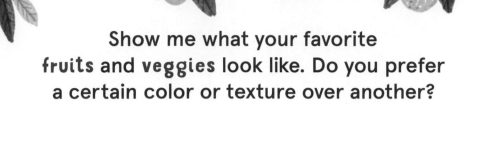

Show me what your favorite
fruits and veggies look like. Do you prefer
a certain color or texture over another?

Foodie Fact!

Each fruit grows differently. Did you know that the more
wrinkled a passion fruit is, the riper and sweeter it is?

WHERE FOOD COMES FROM

Have you ever thought about how those foods got to your kitchen? They took quite the journey to get from the ground to your belly.

Follow the pictures to learn about each food's story!

FARM to GROCERY STORE

SEEDING PLANTING PICKING

WASHING TRUCK to GROCERY STORE

GROCERY UNPACKING LET'S EAT!

Foodie Fact!

Food that's been grown nearby is usually the tastiest, but if you can't get that, frozen or canned food is the next best bet!

PLANTING at HOME

FARM to FARMERS MARKET

I know what you're wondering—how do the fruits and vegetables I eat grow?

Let's start with **SEEDS**.

Sometimes the seeds are small, and there are many of them . . .

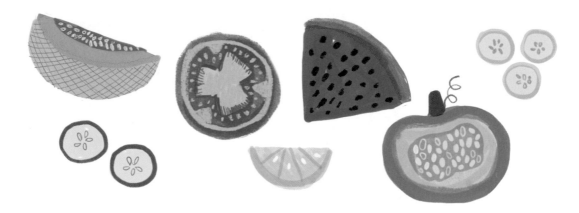

and other times there is only one big **PiT**.

Some foods grow on a **ViNE**...

on a **BUSH**...

on a **TREE**...

or in the **GROUND**.

Foodie Fact!

Not everything starts as a seed. Some plants grow from bulbs or seedpods!

It's so easy that even you can plant
your own seeds at home.

TRY THESE SEEDS!

BELL PEPPERS

APPLES

STRAWBERRIES

TOMATOES

Growing herbs is something you can do on a windowsill.
You can also grow your own avocado or potato plant from a seed.
Plant scallions, celery, and lettuce by placing the bottoms in water
and letting the sun shine on them!

ACTIVITIES

Poke an avocado pit or a potato
with toothpicks, and let part of
it sit in water in the sunshine.
An avocado tree or a potato
plant will grow!

Put scallion, celery, or lettuce bottoms in water, and watch them regrow.

Place a plastic bag over a jar of basil to create a greenhouse steam effect and regrow more basil. Add some water to the jar, and let nature work its magic!

AT-HOME ACTIVITY

Take a tomato seed, and place it in a plastic bag with a moistened paper towel. Tape the bag to a sunny window, and the seed will grow into a little tomato plant!

One thing we all have in common is H_2O!
Water helps everything and everyone grow!
It helps plants, animals, and even YOU grow!

Foodie Fact!

Did you know that every person's body is made up of 60% water? That's what keeps your system running! Just like humans, we superfoods all need water to keep everything moving through our systems. Rain comes down and helps fruits and vegetables grow, just as drinking water helps you!

If you had your own garden, what fruits and veggies would you grow?

Draw them here!

What would you make with the food you grew?

Draw it here!

Did you know that different seasons bring different fruits and veggies?

What is your favorite thing to eat each season?
Can you spot these fruits and veggies in the market stands?

SPRiNG: peas, asparagus, strawberries

SUMMER: watermelons, corn, peaches

FALL: beets, radishes, pumpkins

WiNTER: apples, celery, grapefruit

SPiCES

Foodie Fact!

How well different fruits and veggies grow
depends on what type of climate they're in.

This is how I like to EAT.

My go-to snack
after school is:

_____

The meal I like to eat
on my birthday is:

_____

My favorite things to eat
for lunch are:

_____

I feel the best
when I eat:

_____

Dinner at my house
always starts with:

_____

When I go to my best friend's house,
I always eat:

_____

HOW WE EAT

Eating healthy and cooking do not have to be hard. They're just putting together great ingredients in different ways! The more **fruits** and **vegetables** you eat, the more **vitamins** and **minerals** you put in your body to keep you as healthy as you can be!

So now we know how important it is to team up with our tummy heroes . . . but it's not always easy to think of **HOW** to eat them! There are countless ways to chomp on superpowered fruits and veggies. Here are some ways you can eat them!

RAW

COOKED

FERMENTED

GRILLED

STEAMED

DiPPED

My Superspecial Style:

Draw it here.

Which ways have you tried?

_____

Which would you like to try next?

_____

Now that we know what makes our tummies go YUM, it's time to eat!

Let's visit some families around the world and see how each of them eat. Which one reminds you the most of your family?

IRAN

DENMARK

FRANCE

ITALY

POLAND

COLOMBIA

KOREA

KIMCHI

INDIA

ETHIOPIA

SOUTH AFRICA

ZA'ATAR

ISRAEL

MOROCCO

AUSTRALIA

ACTIVITY:
Set the table for your family!

P S

Now here's something cool! Families in other countries, or people with different heritages, can share mealtimes in really different ways!

Foodie Fact!

I bet you knew that tomatoes are a fruit, but did you know they're the most popular fruit in the WORLD? It's true!

Woo-hoo!

Even the way we serve food can be unique to our home!

Sometimes it can look like this . . .

and other times, it can look like this . . .

or this!

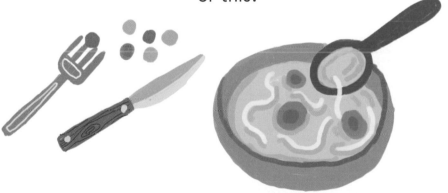

Mealtime is something everyone around the world shares, even if it looks different in every home.

Did you notice what we all have in common?

Some kids have different diets that change the way they fill their plates. Sometimes it's because of an allergy or intolerance, and sometimes it's just a choice that makes their heart happy. Either way, it's totally cool!

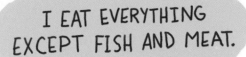

Match each kid to their plate from the buffet!

Vegan

Gluten free

I love to eat everything!

Picky eater

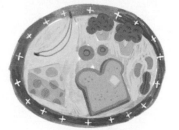

Vegetarian

Pescatarian

I EAT EVERYTHING EXCEPT FISH AND MEAT.

I EAT FISH AS MY MAIN SOURCE OF PROTEIN, AND I ALSO EAT VEGGIES AND GRAINS.

I DON'T EAT WHEAT, BARLEY, OR RYE! BUT I EAT EVERYTHING ELSE.

I DON'T EAT ANYTHING THAT COMES FROM AN ANIMAL (SUCH AS EGGS OR MILK), BUT I LIKE A LOT OF VEGGIES AND GRAINS.

I LET YOU KNOW WHAT I LIKE.

I LOVE TO EAT EVERYTHING!

Let's pick out our favorite vegetables and make something together!

Foodie Fact!

The more color you have in your daily diet, the healthier you will feel!

HERBS:

Basil, mint, rosemary, and turmeric add delicious smells and flavors to any meal! Presto, pasta!

NUTS:

Almonds, cashews, and walnuts come from the earth too! They are neither a fruit nor a vegetable, but they provide lots of healthy fats and protein. They grow both on trees and underground.

OLIVE OIL:

This is excellent for cooking and dipping and drizzling on fruits, veggies, bread . . . and, well, anything!

SEAWEED SNACKS:

These are the best when they're toasted with salt.

MISO:

This seasoning is made from soybeans and adds a delicious fermented flavor to your food.

Wow, I'm getting hungry just looking at all those yummy foods!
Tell me more about how you eat!

My favorite meal of the day is _____.

I like to share mealtime with _____.

Circle the foods you would like to add to your plate!

BREAKFAST

LUNCH

SNACK TIME

DINNER

Foodie Fact!

Try adding olive oil and flaky sea salt
on top of your favorite fruit, and boom—
delicious dessert!

YOU AND FOOD

A healthy body leads to a healthy mind!

CARROTS help your eyes so you can SEE!

LEAFY GREENS like lettuce, spinach, kale, and collard greens help your heart pump blood to keep you moving.

BANANAS help with digestion! They can give you a boost of energy if you're feeling run-down.

When was the last time you went to see the dentist? You know what they say—an apple, carrot, or celery stick a day keeps the cavities away . . . and keeps your breath nice and fresh!

ACTIVITY:

Fruits and vegetables are superheroes, and heroes wear capes!
Let's draw the superpowers these foods have!
What is your dream hero?

DRAW
YOUR OWN!
↙ ↓

Just as a car, a plane, a tuk tuk, or a boat needs energy to work, so do people!

Food is the fuel that helps you stay full and keeps you energized for the day.

Healthy carbohydrates, such as oatmeal, help us stay full.

Greens like spinach have lots of **iron**, which keeps us strong!

Avocados have **healthy fats**, which grease the wheels of our insides and make everything run smoothly.

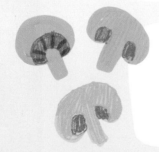

Mushrooms contain **protein**, which sustains our muscles.

It is important to **fuel your body** multiple times during the day to keep yourself moving!

Fruits and **vegetables** do not come with nutrition labels, because when things come from the earth, they are not processed, and they are NATURALLY delicious.

The **fewer ingredients** there are in your food from the grocery store, the better!

Foodie Fact!

Some sugar comes from sugarcane plants! Does that mean it's healthy? Well, it's not so simple. When it comes to sweets, foods that contain processed sugar—such as candies—will just make your belly feel *bleh!*

You truly are what you eat.

If you put junk in your body, you will feel like junk!
What IS junk food, you ask?

When you eat fresh, colorful things from the earth, you will feel as vibrant as the sunshine that helped them grow!

Foodie Fact!

Some of the most popular veggies in China are cabbage, bok choy, potatoes, cucumbers, eggplants, and tomatoes!

My health is important to me!

I eat lots of fruits and vegetables and drink water! Not only do I feel good from putting healthy things into my body, but there are magical powers that go off in my body and mind when I am active. They are called ENDORPHINS!

These are my favorite ways to make endorphins each season:

SPRING

SUMMER

THE FUTURE OF FOOD

The future of food depends on ME, _____!

What you like to eat affects not only you, but also your friends, your family, and the **entire planet**! We can think of it as an ecosystem. Everyone needs to fuel their bodies in order to live. Doing things like recycling and helping the hungry makes everyone's **bellies** and hearts **happier** and more **grateful**.

Did you know that when you grow up, you can have a career working with food? Now that's GOT to be the yummiest job!

My Foodie Future Flow Chart

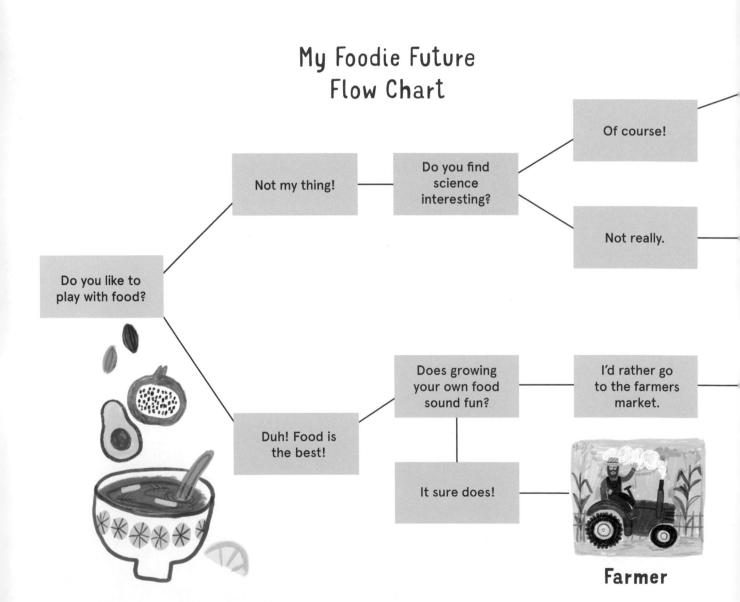

Of course!

Not my thing!

Do you find science interesting?

Not really.

Do you like to play with food?

Does growing your own food sound fun?

I'd rather go to the farmers market.

Duh! Food is the best!

It sure does!

Farmer

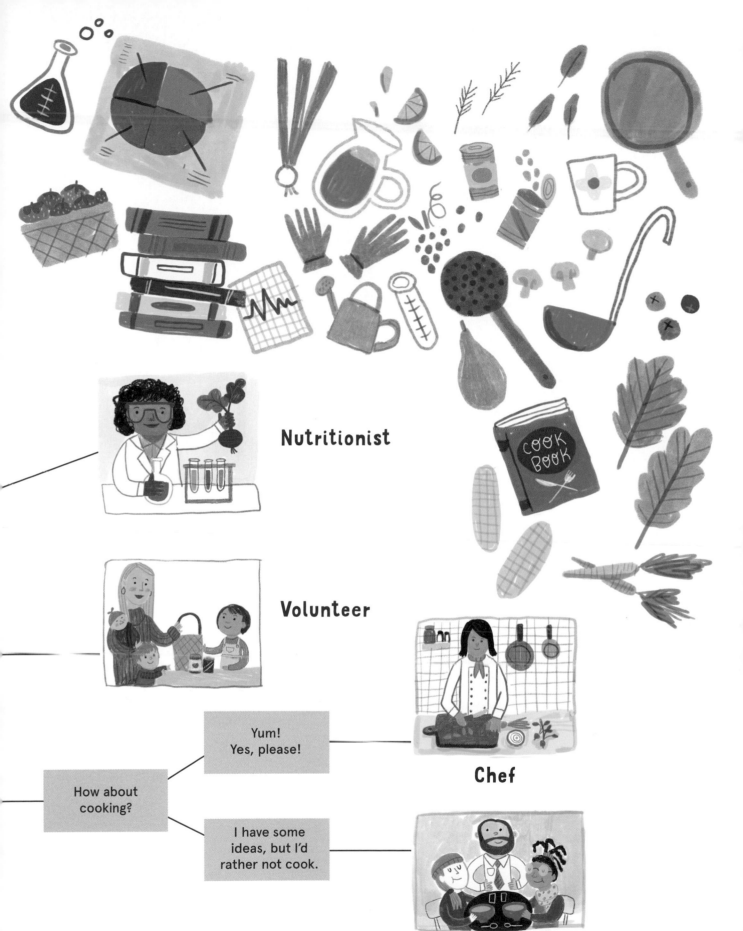

Nutritionist

Volunteer

Chef

Restaurant Owner

Yum!
Yes, please!

I have some
ideas, but I'd
rather not cook.

How about
cooking?

Are there ways you can help people who don't have food to eat?

Some of our fellow humans live in places with a lack of food. These places are called food deserts. There are plenty of ways we can help these people. We know that we humans are all in this together!

Here are some ideas:

Volunteer at a soup kitchen.

Donate food to your local food bank.

Give your family's leftovers to someone in need.

Start a canned food drive at your school.

Volunteer at a community garden.

Foodie Fact!

Did you know that you can use common household items as planters? Cut the top off a plastic water bottle, fill it with dirt, and plant your seeds! Growing your own food doesn't cost much money. It's often just a matter of reusing what you already have.

Fill the community garden with
drawings of fruits and vegetables!

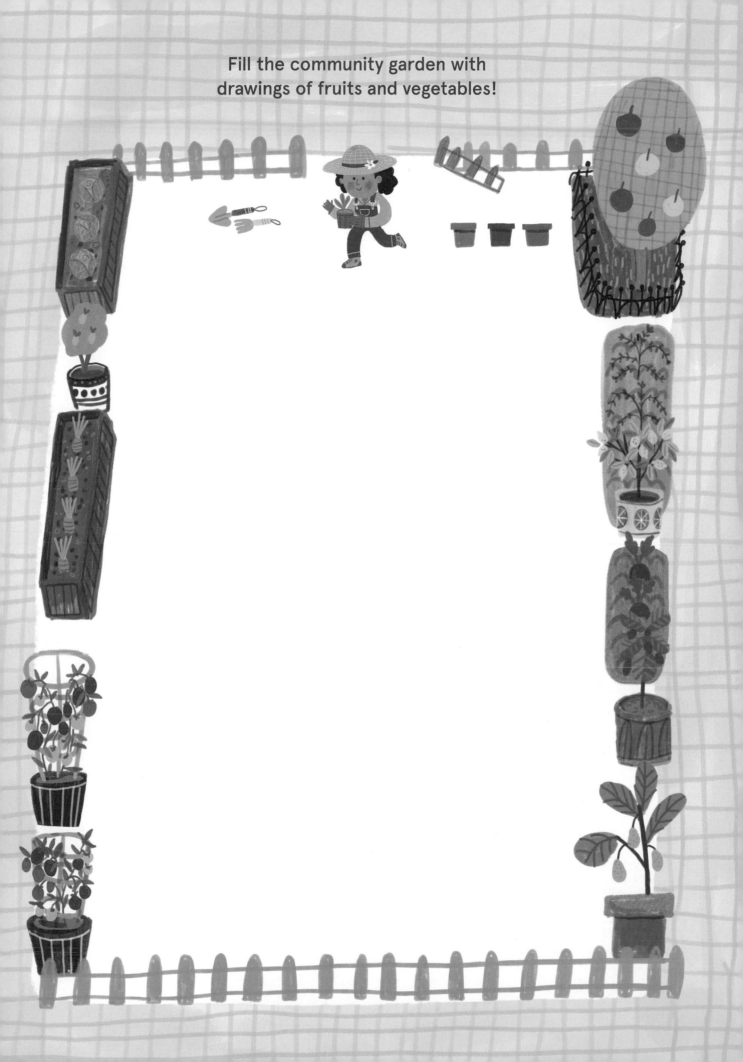

Can I tell you about
something REALLY awesome?
It's called sustainability.

Being sustainable means using all the
resources you have to maintain the
environment. It keeps the world turning!

By recycling and by reusing our
natural resources, like water and soil,
we are able to keep things going
in a natural fashion.

**Find these words on the next page!
You can go across, down, and diagonally.**

COMPOST
RECYCLE
VEGETABLES
FRUIT
VITAMINS
EXERCISE
REUSE
TOMATOES
STRAWBERRY
CARROT

ORANGE
CUCUMBER
SOIL
SUNSHINE
WATER
EARTH
PITS
SEEDS
TREES
APPLE

```
R G O A N G R P S N U H I W R O R C F P
S T R A W B E R R Y J M T K U S Q U R B
V N M X I F O S N V I T A M I N S C H N
S O T A T R J H P N E R W P H X V U A G
U Y C B V U L Z G I P E R O P Y D M C J
T S W T E I M C E C T E V I M L G B R E
V T O M A T O E S N A S N C N V E E E C
E R C I K H W V E U T R E X E R B R U S
G P U G L W Z R E S R P R Z B W Z F S R
E N C E R R Y E D M E B N O R A N G E L
T L E Y E V S E S E C L W K T T M R O K
A K M R I A G B O C Y E G I R E P H S H
B Y T J S B R H R T C M E X E R C I S E
L C O M P O S T P P L O C T U W B L E A
E R L C I J C O H X E J M I A T Y R L O
S M A V M R E W U S T S U N S H I N E B
```

According to the Food and Agriculture Organization (FAO) of the United Nations, more than one billion tons of food are wasted globally each year. That's one-third of all food produced for human consumption! How wild is that?

The best way to reduce food waste is to buy only what you need.

Don't let **LEFTOVERS** go to waste! There are so many people who do not have food. We must remember that and do our best to think about others when we eat and to save what we can. Some meals taste best the next day for lunch.

What do you do with the parts of your fruits and veggies that you don't eat? Waste them? NO! Compost them! Banana peels, apple cores, and potato peels? You can add them to your dirt to make it healthier. Keep a bucket outside with a mix of your dirt, peels, and apple cores. Not only does this make your soil healthier, but it will make fruits and veggies more delicious! If you don't have your own garden, you can take your compost to a composting bin or program in your area.

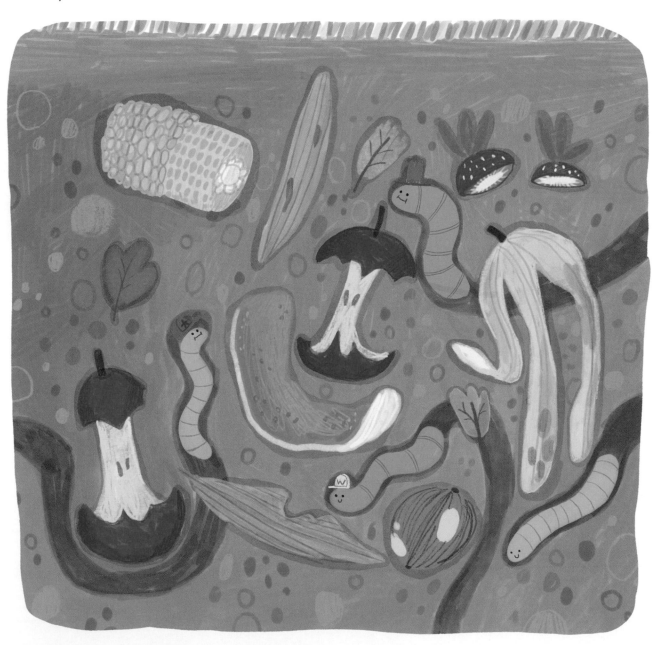

Connect the dots to see what grows from the
COMPOST-ENRICHED SOiL!

Now color them in!

RECYCLiNG is reducing waste by reusing what we can.
Another way to conserve our resources is to turn off our sinks, wells, or other water sources to save water. You can also replant seeds and pits to grow new plants, and you can turn old fruits and vegetables into compost to create healthy soil.

Make it through the maze, avoiding **NONRECYCLABLES**!

START HERE

FINISH HERE

Now that you are a food expert, here are some goals for yourself and your **COMMUNITY**. Check as many as you like!

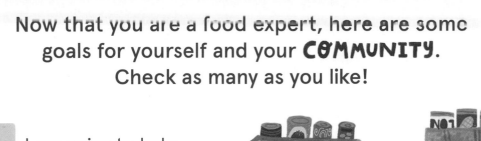

☐ I am going to help set up a canned food drive at school!

☐ I am going to keep some snacks handy to give to those in need.

☐ I am going to try a different-color vegetable or fruit at least once a week!

☐ I am going to go food shopping with an adult.

☐ I am going to learn how to cook!